A Caregiver's Response
Our Shared Journey

—Gary Pacernick—

A Caregiver's Response
Our Shared Journey

ReadersMagnet, LLC

A Caregiver's Response: Our Shared Journey
Copyright © 2020 by Gary Pacernick

Published in the United States of America
ISBN Paperback: 978-1-951775-96-4
ISBN eBook: 978-1-951775-97-1

All rights reserved. No part of this publication may be reproduced, stored in a retrieval system or transmitted in any way by any means, electronic, mechanical, photocopy, recording or otherwise without the prior permission of the author except as provided by USA copyright law.

The opinions expressed by the author are not necessarily those of ReadersMagnet, LLC.

ReadersMagnet, LLC
10620 Treena Street, Suite 230 | San Diego, California, 92131 USA
1.619.354.2643 | www.readersmagnet.com

Book design copyright © 2020 by ReadersMagnet, LLC. All rights reserved.
Cover design by Ericka Obando
Interior design by Shemaryl Tampus

In Memory: Dotti Pacernick (1942-2002)
Beloved Vile, Mother, Grandmother, and Friend

Contents

Acknowledgments 13
Introduction 15

Phase One

Thirty Five Years 18
Phone Call 19
To Whom Should I Pray That Dotti Be Cured 20
First Opinion 21
Second Opinion 22
September 11, 2001 23
Hold Me, Touch Me 24
Anticipation 25
Cat Scan 26
Journey 27
Two Tales In One 28
Pet Scan 29
Five Minutes From The Cancer Clinic 30
Waiting Room Clinic 31
Rite Of Passage 32
Treatment 33
Prognosis 34
Love And War 35
Effects 36
Blood Clot 37

Radiology	38
Overnight	39
Sharing	40
After Surgery To Remove Dotti's Port-O-Cat	41
The Climb	42
Story In The Chemo Room	43
Taking Leave	44
Aftereffects	45
Penultimate Chemo On Christmas Eve	46
High Dose Internal Radiation	47
The Lady In The Wheelchair	48
These Here Herbs	49
Crossing	50
Recovery	51
Post Treatment Exam	52
Checkup With Dr. Chua	53
M.r.i.	54
Waiting	55
Post-Treatment Testing	56
Tapestry	57
Second Post Treatment Checkup With Dr. Simon	58
Yes	60
Tense Talk	61
We're Back	62
The Report	64
Waiting For Still Another Cat Scan	65
Consult After Cat Scan	66
My Angel	68
Father And Daughters	69

Healing 70
What She Says To Me 71
Consult With Dr. Copeland 72
Prayer Poem 74
8 A.M. With Dr. Fowler 75
At The James Cancer Hospital 76

Poem Journal: Phase Two

8/4 Noon Sunday... 78
8/5—1 A.M. Monday 79
7:30 A.M. Monday 80
Noon Monday 81
11 P.M. Monday 82
8/6—9 A.M. Tuesday 83
10:50 A.M. Tuesday 84
12:30 P.M. Tuesday 85
8/7—7:40 A.M. Wednesday 86
12:35 P.M. Wednesday 87
8/8—8:15 A.M. Thursday 88
1 P.M. Thursday 89
8/9—10 A.M. Friday 90
11:30 Friday 91
8/10—9:55 P.M. Saturday 92
8/11—5 A.M. Sunday 93
8/12—9:25 A.M. Monday 94
8/13—12:30 P.M. Tuesday 95
7:25 P.M. Tuesday 96
8/14—8 P.M. Wednesday 97
8/15—5:50 A.M. Thursday 98

2 P.M. Thursday 99
8/16—11:15 A.M. Friday 100
8/17—11:20 A.M. Saturday 101
8/18—9:30 A.M. Sunday 102
8/19—7:45 A.M. Monday 103
3:42 P.M. Monday 104
5:32 P.M. Monday 105
6:10 P.M. Monday 106
Back Home 8/20—8 A.M. Tuesday 107
8/21—7 A.M. Wednesday 108
11 P.M. Wednesday 109
8/22—4:30 P.M. Thursday 110
8/23 Walnut Creek Nursing
    Home—12:15 P.M. Friday 111
7:35 P.M. Friday 112
8/24—11:25 A.M. Saturday 113
11:30 P.M. Saturday 114
8/25—5 P.M. Sunday 115
8/26—7 A.M. Monday 116
6:10 P.M. Monday 117
8:35 P.M. Monday 118
8/27—8:30 A.M. Tuesday 119
8/28—11 A.M. Wednesday 120
8/29 A.M. Thursday 121
8/31—7 A.M. Saturday 122
4:30 P.M. Saturday 123
7:30 P.M. Saturday 124
9/1—1:25 P.M.sunday 125
4 P.M. Sunday 126

9/2—11 A.M. Monday 127
9/3—5 A.M. Tuesday 128
9/4—9 A.M. Wednesday 129
11:15 A.M. 130
9/5—1 P.M. Thursday 131
9/6—8:30 A.M. Friday 132
9/7—8:10 A.M. Saturday 133
3 P.M. Saturday 134
9/8—2 P.M. Sunday 135
9/9—9 P.M. Monday 136
9/10—8:30 A.M. Tuesday 137
9/11—9:10 P.M. Wednesday 138
9/12—3:30 P.M. Thursday 139
9/13—8 A.M. Friday 140
9/14 Saturday 141
9/15 Sunday 142
9/16—6:30 A.M. Monday 143
9/17—3:30 A.M. Tuesday 144
9/18—12:10 P.M. Wednesday 145
9/19—11:15 A.M. Thursday 146
9/20—9:25 A.M.friday 147
9/21 Saturday 148
9/22 Sunday 149
9/23 Monday 150
9/24—8 A.M. Tuesday 151
9/25—2:55 Wednesday 152
5:10 P.M. Wednesday 153
9/26—4:35 P.M. Thursday 154
9/27—10:05 A.M. Friday 155

9/28—7 P.M. Saturday 156
9/29—3:30 P.M. Sunday 157
9/30—9:25 A.M. Monday 158
11:50 A.M. 159

Acknowledgments

I COULD NOT HAVE LIVED through the experience that I write about in these pages without the help of my daughters Jennifer and Eden and their families, and many friends, colleagues, medical personnel, clergy, etc., too many to mention by name. However, I want to especially thank Dotti's sister Geri Taylor and her cousins Carol Nied and Susan Di Giacomo, my sister Judith Parnes, and Rubin Battino, as well as those who read the work in progress: Donald Hall, Philip Levine, Rubin Battino, Jane Baker, and my daughter Eden Sulzer. A special thanks to my partner Peggy Weller for all the positive energy that she has brought to my new life.

Introduction

It never occurred to me that I would outlive my wife Dotti. She was a seminal part of the air I breathed, the flowers I smelled, the fruit I tasted, the flesh I touched, the language I heard. She embodied life as I wished it to be with a woman who accepted me and shared herself with me and made me want to go on to please her: to create a family, make a living, buy and furnish a house, travel and plan for the future. And then one day after thirty three years of marriage the phone rang and her obstetrician gynecologist told her, "You have cancer." Actually, he didn't exactly explain it that way. He said that her latest pap smear showed evidence of several microscopic cancer cells. After she asked several pointed questions, he used the words "invasive cancer." CANCER. The word was so terrifying to me that I was afraid to think it, let alone say it. Now the person whom I loved and had lived with almost my entire adult life had cancer. That's when death became more than a word, a concept, a possibility. Suddenly death in the form of a murderous disease had begun to attack the one person I could not imagine living without. From the moment of that phone call until Dotti's passing took approximately a year. It was a year of tumultuous, terrifying, heartrending events and feelings. It was a year of clinics, hospitals, doctors, nurses, tests, diagnoses, radiation, chemo-therapy, a massive surgery, and then more surgery. It was a year of despair, hope, rage, sorrow, love, and faith. It was a journey that Dotti and I shared as patient and care-giver with our children, nurses, nurse's aides, rabbis, ministers, therapists, friends, relatives, and our five year old grandson. It was and is a journey as life is a journey that always and inevitably involves death. And so death entered our lives. The last year of our time together on earth is what the poems are about. The poems of phase one describe key moments from the early diagnosis through treatment for stage 2A cervical cancer via external and internal radiation and chemotherapy. They also dramatize the terrible moments when we discovered that Dotti's cancer had returned six months after the first round of treatments. This was something we had never dared to contemplate. Dotti suffered through painful even debilitating procedures with the aim of being cured of cancer. We were soldiers on duty during a brief but highly dangerous war against an invisible but deadly enemy. We won the war. At least we thought we won the war. Then just as mysteriously as the cancer surfaced and was destroyed, it recurred. We went from fear and hope to despair and terror. And then to a desperate gamble on a massive surgery called a pelvic exenteration. Although Dotti survived the surgery, she could not finally endure the setbacks and complications that resulted from the operation. The poetry of phase two is concerned with this operation and its aftermath, including Dotti's last days as a hospice patient. Using language to describe, dramatize, and interpret the moment by moment bombardment of events that we experienced is something that I had to do. These poems serve as a being-there in language during the months that Dotti lived and died, my life's partner, whom I wanted to flower forever. During our shared journey I was changed in ways that I would never have imagined; this response is part of an ongoing attempt at healing and hope.

Phase One

DP'S diagnosis and treatment for Cervical Cancer

External and Internal Radiation plus Chemotherapy

Miami Valley Hospital (Dayton, OH); Bathesda North Hospi-tal and Cancer

MiniCenter (Cincinnati, OH); The James Cancer Hospital and Ohio State

University Medical Center (Columbus, OH)

Thirty Five Years

Thirty five years since I first saw Dotti
and her gaze met mine
at the same trajectory
where two strangers
were transfixed
by desire

Thirty five years flash by
and we are back
at that instant
when love's lightning
glance transformed us forever

Phone Call

The phone rings,
Dr. Drollinger,
Dotti's gynecologist,
reporting on her
Leep surgery.

Putting down the receiver,
she is too numb to tell me
what the doctor said.
But I can interpret his message
by reading the fear
in Dotti's eyes.

To Whom Should I Pray That Dotti Be Cured

Should I pray to Yahweh
the Hebrew lord
who can be seen only
at the price of death
but whose hundreds of laws
must be obeyed?
Should I pray to the god
of fate and chance
who cannot be counted on
or to the laws of nature's
inner dynamics
that scientists calculate
as formulas that I cannot
begin to understand?
Maybe I should put my faith
in the doctors with their tests,
procedures, machines, and medicines?
Or should I just bow down
to no one and nothing
and accept what is?

First Opinion

The tall ramrod straight doctor
in the long white starched lab coat
walks into the room and sits
down at the huge table.
Holding clenched hands before him,
he glares at Dotti and says,
"You're wrong. Your cancer is not IA;
it's 1B. You shouldn't pay
attention to the internet."

"But my gynecologist read the report
and said IA," Dotti replies.

He hurls a thick sheath of papers
across the table.
"Here, read the report for yourself.
You need a radical hysterectomy.
That's what standard of care
calls for in your case.
You should be grateful
that we can treat your cancer.
Many women would only wish they had
your chance for a cure.
You're very lucky. Don't be misled
by false information or by those
who speak without knowledge
or authority. Let me know
what you decide."

He stands up,
walks briskly out of the room.

As we hold each other,
Dotti says,
"I'm not letting that man touch me."

Second Opinion

In the small cold gray room
with the window blinds open,
I can see cars flash by
on the road outside the medicenter
while Dr. Simon examines Dotti's cervix.

First, she looks through a long slender scope.
Then she inserts her gloved hand
and moves her fingers over
the whole area. She tells us
that she felt a small knot
that was not detected in Dotti's first biopsy.

I watch her remove three tiny tissue samples.
"I doubt that these will show cancer,
but I want to make sure," the doctor says.
"I'll call you as soon as I get the results."

Driving back to Dayton on the interstate,
I picture Dr. Simon's strong hands,
and I hear her deep resonant voice.
Two days later she tells Dotti
over the phone that the new biopsy
shows that the lesion is cancerous.

Her thoroughness has altered Dotti's diagnosis.
The new treatment plan gives her
a real chance to be cured.
"It will be a long rough road," the doctor says.

September 11, 2001

My wife of thirty three years has cancer.
Soon she starts treatments
to eradicate those secret cells
that terrorize her body
while our country decides how
to counteract those who seek
to destroy our body politic.
Terror breeds terror
from without and from within.
It threatens us all.

Hold Me, Touch Me

As I float on two tall gin and tonics,
Dotti and I sit on the pub's patio
sun beating down.

She eats her red snapper and mashed potatoes
and I my baked trout and brown rice.

She says, "Let's stay out until the sun sets."
We drive to the park and walk around
the sun-speckled pond.
Ducks gliding on the water
promenade on the grassy bank.

An old woman rides by on a bike
with brown and black poodles
in a cage strapped to her rear fender.

When I speak of her illness,
Dotti says, "Hold me, just hold me.
You don't need to talk. just touch.
Touch says everything."

Anticipation

Dotti sits next to me
holding a round monitor
with lights set to shine
when it's her turn
to advance to the next desk.
"Would you mind if I leave
to get my book bag?"
I ask. "I left it in the car."
Lips quivering, she whispers,
"Don't leave me. Don't ever leave me."
I put my arm around her shoulder.
When her monitor sparkles,
we walk to room 12.
While a clerk asks Dotti questions
and types her answers
on an insurance form,
I weep inwardly for both of us.

Cat Scan

Dotti sips a creamy white solution
through a straw.
It will highlight
her stomach and intestines
when the computer reads the x rays
passing through her body.

A soap opera with captions for the deaf
flashes on the TV screen hanging from the wall.
Dotti shows me a brochure
about a spa in Aruba.

A tall slender man
with thinning white hair
in a ponytail
studies the newspaper.

Two black women dressed in white
sit side by side, talking.
In the hallway a man lying on a gurney
curses his medicine.

Dotti begins to cry.
We are being scanned through the dark,
hoping to come Out whole,
holding hands.

Journey

Five days a week for five weeks
I left work,
and .Dotti and I drove down U.S. 75 South
to 275 East to Montgomery
north of Cincinnati.
Here she could get her
radiation and chemo
at the medicenter where her
supervising doctors practiced.

I thought all the driving
would be exhausting,
but it energized me
to be behind
the wheel of our car.
Maybe, just maybe
we could beat the stalking killer
if I could just drive-
drive-drive the damn car.

Two Tales In One

The Pet Scan clinic's
youthful owner
tells me his wife
has thyroid cancer.
He had to take her
to New York for treatment.
Now that they're back home
she has to stay in her motel room
because she's still radioactive.
Meanwhile my wife
lies in the Pet Scan machine;
the x ray lens probing
inside her body.

Pet Scan

While Dotti lies in a dark room,
I sit in a chair scratching
my head with my left hand
and writing this poem
with my right hand,
praying that no brightly lit spots
show up on my wife's pictures
when the radiologist reads them.

Five Minutes From The Cancer Clinic

Cars converge like warring armies
around highway interchanges.
One orange cone blocks the ramp
to our only direct route.
Stopping the car, I get out,
remove the orange cone,
and drive on the ramp.

A tall cop with his
arm and hand outstretched
his eyes masked by sunglasses
runs up to our car
and says, "You've broken the law.
I'm too busy to write a ticket
so just beat it!"

While my wife weeps,
all I can do is return
to the interstate,
drive far south
and double back
to the clinic,
praying that we're not
too late.

Waiting Room Clinic

Ashen-skinned
with hawk-like eyes and beak nose,
he sits with his fingers gripping
the arms of his wheelchair.
Head and back bent,
he inches toward the restroom.
"Shall I push you?"
asks the tall, slender, curly-haired nurse.
Wings beating,
silence grips the air with its talons.

Rite Of Passage

Walking into the chemo room
I see a circle of people
in blue recliners
with chemicals dripping
from clear plastic bags
down through plastic tubes
into their arms, wrists, hands, or chests.
Nurses scurry around
setting up and adjusting
each patient's treatment.
Some sleep; some stare at me
suspiciously
with subterranean eyes,
till they realize
that I am Dotti's companion
in this death-defying rite.

Treatment

Dotti takes eleven medicines
plus radiation and chemotherapy
to counteract the cancer cells
that invaded her body.
It is an all-out war
that she and her doctors
must wage against a deadly foe
that neither knows nor cares
that to Dotti's loved ones
she is irreplaceable
because to us the earth would
be less bearable without her.

Prognosis

Dotti's hands shake
She can't control her bowels
She's so thin her clothes droop
Her skin is pale
Her eyes are downcast
Her smile has disappeared
Her voice is raspy
She feels light-headed and nauseous
Her doctors say her treatment is "going well"
She's "going to be fine"

Love And War

While half the patients in the chemo room,
including my wife,
sleep in their chairs,
others read, talk, and daydream.

On CNN Israel attacks Arafat's headquarters
and U.S. Special Forces and their Afghan allies
prepare to destroy the last
Taliban stronghold in Afghanistan.

An old man breathing with a respirator
asks the blushing oncology nurse
to give him a kiss, and she does.
An act of love amid all this war.

Effects

Today Dotti's energy
and her skin color fade
as the effects of chemo
and radiation set in,
and she aches all over
from carrying her infusion kit.
I massage her legs and feet
and cover her with a blanket
when she sleeps.

Blood Clot

The oncology nurse could not
get a blood draw through Dotti's IV line.
Ninety minutes later
when the blood draw still fails,
the oncology doctor
orders a hospital test.

That night in the hospital
Dotti is put on blood thinners.
When I leave the unit,
the heavy automatic doors
close and lock behind me.

Radiology

While nurses monitor Dotti's vitals,
she lies in bed all night
hooked up to an IV line
dripping blood thinners
through her veins
to bust the clot in her arm.

Nov it's morning and Dotti's
cold and hungry. While she lies
under a huge x ray lens,
two nurses wearing lead-lined clothes
prepare her.

Then the doctor enters the room
and stands beside her.
The picture on the computer screen
shows that Dotti's clot is still there.
The doctor must insert a catheter
in her arm and pump blood thinner
into her vein. She will need to be
monitored closely on the I.C.L7.

I may lose my closest friend,
she with whom
I have broken the glass
into fragments upon the earth.
I will never let her go.
Never never never never never.

Overnight

The nurse brings me a fold-up cot,
a pillow, and linens
so I can stay overnight with Dotti
while blood thinner drips
into her veins, and her vital signs
zigzag across a monitor.

All night the hallway stays lit,
and a nurse keeps checking on Dotti.
Although I may sleep fitfully,
we rest close to each other,
hearing each other's breathing.

Sharing

In the fifth floor hospital lounge,
a woman offers to share
her supper with me.

"Too much for me to finish," she says.
Her husband's cancer
has spread to his liver;
the tumor mass is huge.

"His pulse rate is 166," she says,
shaking her head.
"People are praying for us day and night
in our prayer group,
so he should be fine.
If not, then it's God's will,
and I accept that,
because God's watching over us."

After Surgery To Remove Dotti's Port-O-Cat

While Dotti is wheeled to her room.
I meet with the surgeon,
who says that she is fine.
Her port had pulled out of the catheter
and worked its way back to her heart.
Dotti says that she has
a splitting headache
and feels nauseous
from the anesthetic.
She dabs her forehead
with a cold wet cloth.
Her face is a dripping wet mask.

The Climb

While Dotti sits in her blue recliner
with an IV line stuck in her vein,
I climb the hill above the medicenter
and sit on a bench
soaking up sunlight.

Two nurses on lunch break
walk briskly by me and down the hill.
A white truck with "Peter Gregory Florist"
painted on its side pulls up
to the hospital receiving area and stops.

A woman with a ponytail flapping
behind her cap jumps out,
carrying flowers for some patient
confined to the hospital
as Dotti was two weeks ago.

Now the Document Destruction company's
"On-Site Confidential Data
and Material Destruction" truck drives up.
I decide to move on
before the shredding starts.

Walking slowly down the hill
back to the medicenter
where Dotti sits
in her blue recliner,
I wonder if she misses me.

Story In The Chemo Room

"Had a tumor in my chest
seven to ten centimeters,"
says the bald toothless man
with eyes like brown marbles.
"Didn't know it was there.
The doctors found it.
Said if it got bigger
it would burst
and that would be it for me.
I'm seventy five. Can't complain.
How much more time do I have?
Just couldn't live with the uncertainty.
Said go ahead. Take it out.
The operation almost killed me.
Now they're giving me chemo.
Doing whatever they can
to keep me alive.
But I'm happy.
Had a large family.
Six grandchildren.
Two greatgrandkids.
Too bad you can't just
wave a magic wand.
Make everything better.
But that's not how it works.
Is it?"

Taking Leave

The tiny gray-haired lady
with flashing green eyes
says she smoked and drank for years
until cancer caught up with het.

In the chemo room,
her husband and I
have sat next
to our wives for weeks
breathing each others' pain and fear.
Now we are giddy with laughter.

Our wives sit in their recliners
with IV lines in their veins.
They are partners in adversity
sharing a few last words
before lights turn off
and doors lock.

Aftereffects

Dotti doesn't want
the quarter pounder with cheese
she requested
from MacDonald's
because she has to
excrete the fluids
that hydrate her
during chemotherapy.
When she returns to her recliner,
she says she almost threw up
and fainted in the restroom.
After taking her temperature,
the lithe blond nurse brings her
a can of pop and a bag of pretzels,
but she's fast asleep.

Penultimate Chemo On Christmas Eve

I sit next to Dotti watching
the slow drip of fluids
down the plastic tube into her vein.

Across the room the radiation oncologist
kisses an almost comatose patient;
her eyes closed, her scalp almost bald.

Escorted by his youthful attendant,
the slender, olive-skinned man in the wheel chair
tells me he likes the cut of my sports jacket.

He says they don't know how to stop
his cancer from spreading through his body.
"Yes, I smoked. I was a bad boy."

He has a commanding voice and sparkling eyes.
I watch his nurse push him
down the hallway to a private room.

The tiny old lady who wears a gray turban
says she can't wait to get home
and start cooking Christmas dinner.

The nurse disconnects Dotti's IV.
It's almost time to drive toward
brightly shining Christmas lights.

High dose internal radiation

It's sixty five degrees in December
as we drive through pouring rain
to Dotti's third high dose
internal radiation treatment.

When we arrive at the clinic,
a nurse takes Dotti into a room
and closes the door.
For over two hours I wait
for her procedure to end.

Finally, the rail-thin youthful doctor
with long brown hair and big child-like eyes
stands in the waiting room doorway.
"Your wife's doing just great."
"What are her chances for a cure?" I ask.
"Fantastic," she replies.
"Thanks. That's great,
but I wish she could be happy."

"She will be happy five years from now,"
the doctor says. I watch her
return to the room and close the door.

The Lady In The Wheelchair

The skinny, red-haired lady with glasses
sits in her wheelchair
and says she's the only one
in her building who does anything.
The others lie around and complain;
even though they're able-bodied.
She's had a terminal neurological disease
for over twenty years
and now she has to get radiation
to treat her breast cancer.
"You just have to keep going," she says.
"Keep active, don't ever give up.
I've been there at least four times
in that deep black hole,
and each time I got spit out.
Faith's the most important thing.
You've got to believe that God
will always be there for you."
When the intercom calls her name,
she says, "So long" and speeds away
in her motorized wheelchair.

These Here Herbs

The nonstoptalking lady in curlers
bellows in the waiting room,
"Cancer is caused by what you eat.
All this here medical stuff
won't help a fly
let alone a person.
Why all you got to do is take
these here herbs that are listed
in this here catalogue."
She pulls it out of her purse
and waves it in the air.
"Don't you want to see it?"
she asks the heavyset lady
seated across from her.
"I take them herbs sometimes,"
the lady replies,
"but only in addition to medical treatments.
I wouldn't put all my trust
in just them herbs."
"You read this catalogue.
These here herbs are guaranteed.
Ain't no medicine can compare with them.
They got jungle magic
can cure an elephant
let alone a human being."

Crossing

I lie here thinking of you
my precious one my princess
my one and only woman
with whom I crossed a stormy sea
toward the calm harbor
while the red star
slowly set in the west.

Recovery

The person who Dotti was
before her diagnosis
has reentered her face and body
shines through her eyes
moves quickly gracefully
smiles laughs speaks
of her renewed desires and hopes
all that she has endured
fades into cracks and crevices
where she no longer wishes to be
as she bursts into sunlight

Post Treatment Exam

Partially covered by a sheet
Dotti lies back on the exam table
with her legs spread apart
and her feet in stirrups.
Dr. Simon leans down and looks
through a scope at Dotti's cervix.
"It's gone," she says.
"There's no sign of the tumor."

She removes the scope.
"You'll feel some pressure now."
Inserting her hand into Dotti's womb,
she moves her fingers over some tissue.
"Beautiful. The radiation and
chemotherapy did their work."
"What about recurrence?" I ask.
"The cure rate is sixty to seventy per cent."

Then she turns to Dotti and smiles.
"Now it's time for you to get your life back.
I'll see you in six weeks
for a pap smear."

When I ask her to explain
her cure rate figures,
she replies, "I've already answered
your question" and leaves the room.

It's the same room where she
found Dotti's tumor, and we started
down what the doctor called
"that long rough road."

Checkup With Dr. Chua

Tiny, black haired, sylph-like Dr. Chua,
Dotti's medical oncologist, says
she can stop taking coumadin to thin her blood.

That means Dotti doesn't need to
have her blood drawn and tested
each week to measure
her red and white blood cell count.
Her mammogram and pap smear
were negative, but her Cat scan
showed a cyst on her ovary
and a low density area on her cervix.

Dr. Chua says that the cyst
is most likely benign,
and the low density area
could be caused by drainage.

"All in all you're doing fine," says Dr. Chua.
She tells us that not all patients
with cervical cancer respond to treatment.
"Then what happens?" Dotti asks.

"One of our patients who still had a tumor
after radiation and chemotherapy
has been in the hospital for weeks
and had to have extensive surgery."
"I always told myself that my treatment
would be successful," Dotti responds.
"If I believed there was a real chance for failure,
that would have been too terrifying."

M.R.I.

Dotti lies still for two hours
in this long, tube-like machine.
Sitting outside the dark room
a technician watches pictures
of her organs—planets whirling—
on multiple computer screens.
He says she should know the results
in twenty four hours.

A week later Dotti still waits.
Finally, the phone rings.
The doctor's nurse says
the results were not conclusive.
The radiologist could not identify
a dark mass on Dotti's ovary.
Her doctor wants her to have
more NIRI pictures taken.
Once more she must enter
the machine's belly
for one more attempt to probe
her body's shadowy secrets.

Waiting

Dotti is waiting for the phone to ring
waiting to pick up the receiver
and hear someone's voice tell her the results
of her latest test   the terror of not knowing
and not wanting to hear the dreaded words
Waiting for the phone to ring
waiting to pick up the receiver
to hear someone's voice speak the words
that she doesn't want to hear
the terror of not knowing.

Post-Treatment Testing

First Dotti had a Pap Smear
and then a pelvic exam,
followed by a CAT scan,
which showed something on her ovary.
She waited and waited and heard nothing.
Then she was told to get an MRI.
Even that test proved inconclusive
because the radiologist could not identify
a dark mass on her ovary.
So she had to have more MRI pictures.
After six weeks of tests and waiting,
the radiologist ruled that
the mysterious mass was
a non-cancerous fibroid.
Even now she fears the phone
will ring and she will hear
MORE BAD NEWS.

Tapestry

If there is meaning
in Dotti's suffering,
it requires
faith beyond the mind's
quest for certainty.
It is as if light and dark,
hope and dread,
life and death
are intertwined
in a tapestry
too complex
to unravel.

Second Post Treatment Checkup With Dr. Simon

"Lie back," says Dr. Simon,
as she adjusts her round light beam.
Dotti's feet rest in metal stirrups
covered by large oven gloves;
her legs are spread apart.
Dr. Simon peers into her womb.
Then she puts her gloved hand inside
and moves it over the tissue.
"You'll feel some pressure.
Try to relax your muscles."

After she removes her hand,
Dr. Simon takes off the yellow plastic glove
and drops it on the floor.
"It looks quite different than
the last time 1 examined you.
There's a gray area that concerns me.
It may be deterioration
caused by the radiation.
It's hard to say. We go by images.
If I want to be more exact,
I'd have to take a biopsy
and that poses its own risks.
I can't rule out a tumor,
but I don't believe that's it.
Now if you'll get dressed,
I'll be right back. I want to
take a look at this slide."

Dotti dismounts from the table
and slowly put on her clothes.
"You have a vaginal infection,"
says Dr. Simon, reentering the room.
"I'm prescribing a salve
that you inject with an applicator.
Then I want to see you
in two or three weeks.
We should have the results
of the pap smear by then."

After the doctor leaves the room,
Dotti says, "I feel at peace
and I don't know why.
This whole thing started months ago
when Dr. Simon found scar tissue
and felt a small knot.
She took three punch biopsies
just to be sure it wasn't cancer.
Sure enough, on September 11
she called and told me the biopsy
showed that I had cancer."

Yes

When I approach the side door,
I see Dotti through the glass.
Walking toward me,
she hesitates, wavers;
her eyes seem faraway.
Opening the door,
I enter, step toward her.
"What's wrong?" I ask.
"Let's go sit down," she says.
"Dr. Simon called.
She said the pap test
showed possible evidence
of squamous cancer cells.
She can't be sure
until she does a biopsy
and the results come back."
Dotti's eyes begin to water.
"Damn," I say. "Damn. Damn. Damn."
Then I bring Dotti close to me,
hold her in my arms,
and hear her say,
"We have to be strong for each. other."
Yes. I say yes to myself. Yes.

Tense Talk

Our older daughter calls.
When I tell her about her mother's pap test,
there is silence between us,
as well as a long highway ride.
"It's lousy news," I say,
"But we have to face it.
What else can we do?"
Still no response. Dotti picks up the phone.
"Your dad and I are being brave.
We have to be there for each other.
We can't let this tear us apart.
We won't know anything for sure
until the biopsy report comes back."
Getting on the phone again,
I tell her not to worry, though I know
she will, and I feel guilty
for having told her about the pap test.
"I love you both," she whispers
before she hangs up the phone.

We're Back

Back in the same room
with the black shades drawn
where Dr. Simon took the biopsy
that showed a cancerous knot
on Dotti's cervix. We're back
because her second post-treatment
pap test showed signs of cancer cells.
While her feet rest in stirrups,
Dotti leans back on the examining table
and speads her legs apart.
Dr. Simon looks through her scope
to inspect her pelvic area.
Then Dr. Simon inserts her gloved hand
and feels all over and around Dotti's tissue.
"It's like wall board," she says.
"It's going to be hard to get good samples
because the radiation has
caused so much damage.
With her assisting nurse at her side,
Dr. Simon inserts her long
metal snipping instrument
and slowly removes six samples,
which the nurse carefully
puts in plastic containers.
"This may show evidence of
a very stubborn tumor," the doctor says.
"There's no reason—given the very
aggressive treatment that you got—
that it should have come back so soon."

"So it's scary," I blurt out.
"Yes, it's very scary," she replies.
"We'll have to wait and see.
My guess is that the biopsy
may not be definitive.
I may have to do additional
needle biopsies. You would be
under a general anesthetic.
It would be done in the hospital.
I would never expect you to
have it done here in these conditions."
"What are the chances that
the radiation damage has caused
the pap test to show cancer cells?" Dotti asks.
"Fifty-fifty," replies Dr. Simon.
When I leave the examining room
to return to the waiting area,
my head begins to feel light,
and I start to faint,
a circus of horrors
spinning around my head.

The Report

Around 4 P.M. the phone rings.
I run to it by instinct,
pick up the receiver,
and hearing Dr. Simon's voice
exclaim, "Oh no. Please no.
DON'T TELL ME."
But I can't help hearing her say
that Dotti's biopsy showed cancer.
What we dreaded is now a fact.
"I hate to have Dotti scanned some more,"
the doctor says, "but we
need to have it done
so we can see
where the cancer is,
and then we will meet
and talk about options."
"Okay?" she asks. "Okay."
"My nurse will call and set up
an appointment for a CAT scan.
I'll be on call all weekend
if Dotti wants to talk with me."

Waiting For Still Another Cat Scan

The TV monitor on the wall over my head
shows romantic land and seascapes
and plays slow, haunting melodies.
In the hall outside the waiting area,
an old gray-haired woman on a gurney
breathes portable oxygen
while hooked up to an IV unit.
Her eyes closed, her hands clasped
in her lap, she slowly moves her head.
I hear seagulls squawking
and bells ringing from the TV sound track.
Seated near me are a young man and woman.
She jiggles her foot over her knee,
and he stares straight ahead.
They are holding hands, their fingers interlocked.
A technician calls out, "Dotti Pacernick."

Consult After Cat Scan

In the gray-walled exam room, Dr. Simon
does Dotti's pelvic exam and finds
no evidence of new cancer.
She then explains that the CAT scan
showed no further spreading of cancer,
but that doesn't mean it isn't there.
It may just be too small to show up.

"You have three options," she says,
"and none of them are good.
You can do nothing. You can try to slow
the tumor's growth through chemotherapy,
or you can have a pelvic exenteration.
It's a radical operation. Only one in four
candidates qualifies for it.
There is a ten percent risk of death
from the operation. If you survive,
the cure rate is only about thirty percent."

Dotti asks why the treatment worked
for six months, and then the cancer came back.
"Rotten luck," replies Dr. Simon.
"Goddamnit," I say. "Yes. Goddamnit,"
the doctor responds, her coal-black eyes
peering at me. "Look, if you're thinking
malpractice, you don't have a leg to stand on."

"You found the cancerous knot,
and that changed Dotti's diagnosis.
Knowing what you do now, would you still
do the radiation and chemotherapy
instead of a radical hysterectomy?"
"Yes," she says. "The cure rate is the same:
sixty to seventy percent, but we can't
guarantee a cure. There's always risk.
With the 2A staging Dotti had the right treatment."
"Case closed," I reply, extending my hand to the doctor.

My Angel

Seeing Dotti asleep on the sofa
her hands in prayer position
pointed toward her chin
I would kiss her
but don't want to awaken her.

Father And Daughters

Jennifer, Eden, and I
walk up and down hills.
Each of us is thinking of Dotti
their mother and my wife:

How we must wait and hope
for her latest test results
for her new treatment plan
for the second opinion.

For whatever happens
each of us is near the other
step by step holding hands
walking over the earth.

Healing

If I could emulate Jesus' faith healing,
I would place my hands
upon my love's shoulders
look deeply into her eyes
and speak the words
"Now you are healed,
and now you may go forth
whole and happy in the world
for the rest of your days."
Light would shine from her eyes
at the miracle of her renewed health.
I would bow and kiss the earth
and give thanks to the creator.

What She Says To Me

You can save me.
When you set your mind
to something, you accomplish it.
You are powerful with words
and with who you are.
Your love is immeasurable to me.
The doctors cannot measure
the human spirit
and miracles do happen.
Your love fills me with hope.

Consult With Dr. Copeland

Jennifer, Dotti, and I drive ninety miles
through blistering heat to Camelot Women's Center.
Eden joins us from Clevehnd.
Then we wait for over two and a half hours
until the doctor is ready to meet with us.

Although he has seen patients all day,
he appears rested and immaculate
in his white shirt, tie, and starched white lab coat.
Even his bald scalp shines.

While he surveys a file of Dotti's scans,
biopsies, and other medical reports,
he asks questions, pursing his lips
and wrinkling his brow.
Setting aside Dotti's medical file,
he says that in his opinion
she is a candidate
for a pelvic exenteration.

Using a set of medical charts,
the doctor shows us how
the operation will eliminate
all of Dotti's pelvic organs
and involve two ostomies.

He explains that first Dotti will be
opened up and examined to find out
if her cancer has spread. If it has not,
then the operation can proceed.

At 7:30 P.M. we leave the cancer center
and say goodby to Eden.
Halfway to Dayton, Dotti suffers
severe pain and a panic attack.

We stop at a MacDonald's so she can
get a cup of water and swallow her pain pills.
Reaching home, she can rest until tomorrow
when she must make a momentous decision.

Prayer Poem

May you sleep soundly, my love.
May you find a respite from
the enemy that defied
your doctors' treatment plan,
returning to plague you.
But you will not relent
in your struggle to survive.
Tomorrow you meet the surgeon
who will perform an operation
that could cure you.
Athough there are grave risks,
you accept them, because you
are not ready to leave your loved ones,
just as we cannot bear to lose you.
May you sleep soundly, my love.
May you gain solace and strength
for the challenges that you must face.

8 A.M. With Dr. Fowler

Dr. Fowler is slender, bearded, youthful.
'Smiling, he explains the operation
that he will perform on Dotti
if her cancer has not spread too far.
He uses charts and drawings
to show how he will proceed.
Then he discusses the options
for reconstructive surgery.

We all know that this terrible operation
is Dotti's only hope for a cure.
Leaving the air-conditioned clinic,
we feel the blazing heat.

At The James Cancer Hospital

Dotti's radiologist is a slender, bleak-eyed
Indian doctor who speaks with a lisp.
Because she is in so much pain,
she begs him not to examine her.

Because Dotti's extreme pain persists,
the nurse consultant comes
to our room in radiology.

A tiny, dark-complected woman,
she speaks in a near whisper.
She tells us that she is a survivor
of cervical cancer, which she contracted
when she was a nursing student.

Besides giving us our first lesson
in applying and removing stomas,
she marks Dotti's body with a felt pen
to show the surgeon where to make
the openings for Dotti's stomas.

"I felt terrible when I had cancer
until I found peace
and could just let it go."
When I ask her what she means,
she says, "I gave myself up to the lord."

Poem Journal: Phase Two

Pelvic Exenteration: The James Cancer Hospital

8/4 NOON SUNDAY

While Dotti's computerized pump
activates her IV drip,
she sleeps in her recliner
waiting for the angiogram
that will test her blood vessels
in preparation for her surgery.
The firefighter-paramedic
in the next recliner
is getting a transfusion
to increase his red blood cell count.
His lymphoma has recurred,
and he needs a stem cell transplant.
"I need to talk," he says.
"I hope you don t mind.
If I didn't have someone
to talk to, I'd go crazy."

8/5—1 A.M. MONDAY

After 1 A.M. Dotti's bowels
are clear, and she can stop
drinking Go-Lightly and try to sleep.
Resting on the cot
next to her hospital bed,
I doze on and off, arising at 5 A.M.
At 5:30 her team
of attending residents and students
gathers outside her door
to greet her before surgery,
but Dotti can't leave the bathroom.

7:30 A.M. MONDAY

The operating room's
waiting area is flooded
with fluorescent light.
Eden puts two warm blankets over Dotti,
who asks to see Dr. Fowler, her surgeon.
He appears and tells her that he
will first have to determine
if the operation can go forward.
We shake hands.
Then Eden and I must leave Dotti.

NOON MONDAY

Sitting with many others
in the huge atrium family waiting area,
Eden and I take turns dozing.
Three hours after Dotti left us,
the receptionist comes to bring us
to the phone at her desk.
Dotti's operating room nurse
says that because no cancer
was found in Dotti's lymph nodes
the operation will proceed.
I want to believe that
this is all a dream
and I will soon wake up.

11 P.M. MONDAY

Dressed in green scrubs,
his head covered by
a polkadot paper net,
Dr. Fowler meets Eden and me
in the partially lit hospital lounge
with the illuminated aquarium.
He says that closing Dotti up
presented big problems
because she is so tiny
and her body was so swollen with fluids.
He had to leave her wound partly open,
but he hopes that she will heal over time.
Otherwise he is happy
because the tumor is gone.
The lights in the aquarium are off.
I cannot see the fish.
Where am I? Who am I?

8/6 — 9 A.M. TUESDAY

I enter the labyrinthine surgery
intensive care unit
and find Dotti in bed D33.
Her face and arms are bloated
to twice normal size.
She has a tube in her mouth
and another tube in her nose.
Her eyes are dilated, opaque,
and caked with wax,
but her right hand squeezes
my right hand and won't let go.
Feeling nauseous and dizzy,
I sit back, still holding her hand.

10:50 A.M. TUESDAY

Dr. Cohn says Dotti is very alert.
She's been through a lot
but she is doing very well.
During her twelve hour operation
her surgical and radiology teams
got all the cancer, and she can
look forward to being cured
of the disease that has hounded her.
Despite my dread, I try
to believe his words.
I am blinded by
fluorescent lights.

12:30 P.M. TUESDAY

Dotti writes frantically
because she can't speak.
"Find out about liability.
They did four ostomies
instead of two.
You must get Dr. Fowler."

After the nurse and technician
remove her breathing tube,
Dotti chokes and gags for many minutes.

Later she writes, "I want YOU ONLY
to stay with me tonight
even if you have to stay on another floor.
It's very important to me."
She pounds her fist on the pad
and hands it to me.

8/7—7:40 A.M. WEDNESDAY

Jenny and I find Dotti
in D33 of the Surgery ICU.
Dotti is very agitated.
She keeps complaining
about her pain. "It's all over.
Around my back, my stomach,
my arms, my legs.
I feel like crap. It's as if
I've been run over by a truck
is how I'd put it."

jenny tells her, "The hospital staff
is doing an excellent job
of caring for you.
You need to rest
and try to stop imagining
conspiracies against you
by the doctors and nurses.
No one is giving you a kidney transplant.
There is no liability issue, mom."

12:35 P.M. WEDNESDAY

Since Dotti sleeps
while Eden watches her,
I find the TV lounge
and lie down on a sofa,
curling my legs over the arm.
CNN HEADLINE NEWS reports
about a twenty two hour operation
to separate Siamese twins.
While I try to read a magazine,
some stranger sleeps on another sofa.

8/8—8:15 A.M. THURSDAY

Two nurses and I help Dotti
get off her bed and into a chair.
She is filled with mucous
that she can't spit out.
"I feel like I've been run over
by a big bus," she says.

1 P.M. THURSDAY

Mary the ostomy nurse
a short, stocky, gray-haired woman
with huge emerald eyes
and a tiny ponytail,
takes off Dotti's dressings,
and removes and replaces
her colostomy and urostomy bags,
all the while demonstrating
the key steps in the process
of using Dotti's new plumbing.
"It's not hard," she says.
"You just have to learn the basics."
Dotti's eyes are closed.

8/9—10 A.M. FRIDAY

"I can't compete with Eden,"
I say to Dotti.
"She's the perfect daughter,
the perfect person.
I've always rubbed you the wrong way.
I know that you prefer Eden."
"I should have died," Dotti replies.
"I can't survive this horrible surgery
without your love. How can you
be vicious to such a sick person?
I can't take it. I'll just die."
"Do you want me to leave?"
"No. That would be worse."
"Please forgive me and I'll stay."
"I forgive you." We embrace.
She smiles. We shake hands.

11:30 FRIDAY

As nurses and technicians
in green, blue, and white scrubs
leave the hospital on shift change,
I stare at the statue of Hope,
a tall, graceful maiden lifting a torch skyward.
A young man in t-shirt, khakis,
and a white cap cradles
a tiny puppy in his arms.

I sit on a gnarled gray bench
surrounded by giant shade trees.
While I think of Dotti attached
to an IV line, drains, and stomas,
the earth is dappled by sunlight.

8/10—9:55 P.M. SATURDAY

Dotti demands that I stay overnight
with her in her hospital room
because she is afraid.
"A Enid of what?" I ask.
"What's more important than staying
with your wife of 34 years?
Where else would you rather be?"

8/11—5 A.M. SUNDAY

The lord is my shepherd
I shall not wallow in self-pity
because of my wife's illness and surgery
and the pain that she must bear
and that I must witness,
feeling terrified and helpless
as my world spins out of control.

8/12—9:25 A.M. MONDAY

After spending the night with Dotti,
Eden leaves, and I help Dotti
move from her bed to a chair.
When she tells me that she is in pain,
I buzz for the nurse,
but no one comes, and when
I walk to the nurses's station
to request attention for Dotti,
her young blond nurse glares at me.
Minutes later she arrives
with Dotti's pain medicine.
Then a technician appears
to take an x ray of Dotti's bowel.
Moving from her chair
back to her bed, pain grips
Dotti's face as she lies on her back
and the x ray is snapped.
Then after Dotti's bath
with washcloth, soap, and water,
she sits by the sink
dabbing herself with
deodorant and skin cream.

8/13—12:30 P.M. TUESDAY

Asleep for two hours, Dotti awakes
and demands to leave her bed
to go to the bathroom.
"But you have an ostomy bag,
so you don't have to do anything."
"I want to sit on the toilet."
"What will that accomplish?"
"At least I'll have some privacy."
Two nurses rush in.
"It's not unusual for ostomy patients
to want to sit on the toilet,"
says one of the nurses.
Dotti has already asked me to leave the room
but where can I go? What can I do?
I who have been Dotti's caregiver
since she was diagnosed with cancer
wonder how she who chose
radical surgery to save
her life can survive
the trauma of living.

7:25 P.M. TUESDAY

Returning from the cafeteria
with cake and coffee on a tray,
I hear Dotti screaming "Help, help"
and see a nurse's aide
trying to calm her down.
"What's wrong?" I ask her.
"I was trapped in the chair
and couldn't find the nurse's button.
You left me alone."
"For ten minutes? I can't believe this."
"I want my pain medicine.
I hurt all over. The doctors say
that my pain needs to be controlled.
I need to go to the bathroom."
"But you can't go to the bathroom.
You have two ostomies.
They're giving you medicine to try
and get rid of your gas.
You need to walk and use your breathing device."
"I need my pain medicine now."
"Then call the nurse," I reply.

8/14—8 P.M. WEDNESDAY

Thank you Donna Sulzer
Eden's mother-in-law
for spending a day with Dotti
and bringing your homemade
German chocolate cake
to share with us and the staff.
Thank you Donna Sulzer
for being a sweet, compassionate woman.
I was touched when you said
that your cake with DOTTI
inscribed with blue icing
was to celebrate the Happy Birthday
of Dotes new life.

8/15—5:50 A.M. THURSDAY

Walking to the hospital
I cross the bridge over the river
reflecting shadows
of surrounding trees.
Tall buildings loom on the horizon
waiting to swallow me.

2 P.M. THURSDAY

The fat physical therapist
takes Dotti for a walk,
holding on to her
with a belt attached to both of them.
Dotti climbs six stairs
though her skin is ghost-white
and each step hurts her.

8/16—11:15 A.M. FRIDAY

I pick up jenny at the airport.
With her high cheekbones,
big green eyes and dark, curly hair
she is Dotti incarnate.
She and I. are young women
who carry their mother with them.
I could not endure Dotti's terrible
fight to survive without them.
All of us wonder whether
we can go on without Dotti.

8/17—11:20 A.M. SATURDAY

Two medical students
remove Dotti's sutures with tiny pliers
and put tape over her wounded skin.
In two weeks she has come through
a massive surgery to destroy a tumor
spreading throughout her pelvis
that threatens to kill her.

Sleep in your bed, my angel,
and when you awake,
you will begin to lead
your miraculous new life.

8/18 — 9:30 A.M. SUNDAY

Dotti still can't fully empty and reclamp
her colostomy bag, so some watery shit
spills on the bathroom floor.
When I groan and grimace,
Dotti says I'm being sarcastic,
always hovering, always
trying to control her.
Feeling scared, helpless, hurt,
I want to leave her,
but where in the world
would I go without hating myself?

8/19—7:45 A.M. MONDAY

Dotti tells me she had an accident.
Trying to clean her colostomy bag,
she lost control, and her feces spilled
on the bathroom floor.
Although she rang for help,
no one came until
her chief resident
found her and took control.
Dotti says that her face
was contorted during the ordeal.

3:42 P.M. MONDAY

Although Dotti's medical team
has told us that she will be released today,
her orders have still not
shown up on the computer,
so I help her back in bed.
She falls soundly asleep.

5:32 P.M. MONDAY

The medical student comes
to discharge Dotti from the hospital.
As she drinks water and eats a cookie,
I write down words in my notebook.

6:10 P.M. MONDAY

While the nurses empty Dotti's ostomy bags
and dress her in her own clothes
for the first time in many days,
I wait outside, breathing fresh air.
The black nurse's aide wheels Dotti
to our car, and with her help
Dotti maneuvers into the front seat.
The car is packed. We are
ready to return to our house.

Back Home 8/20—8 A.M. TUESDAY

After I drained Dotti's bags
and hooked her up
to a bedside drain,
she slept through the night.
This morning we are
both awakened by roofers
lipping old shingles off our roof.
I haven't had much love in my life,
certainly not from my parents,"
Dotti says, white-faced
from her bed of pain.
"Just tell me you love me.
That's all I want to hear."

8/21—7 A.M. WEDNESDAY

At 7 A.M. Dotti gets out of bed
and falls on her way to the bathroom,
though I told her she did not need
to empty her bags
and certainly not on her own.
"Stop yelling at me," Dotti says.
Eden urges me to get a private duty nurse.

11 P.M. WEDNESDAY

Dotti wets her nightgown,
complains of pain,
and seems delirious,
so I call the emergency night nurse.
An hour later I flag her down on our street
since she can't find our house in the dark.
The nurse changes Dotti's urostomy bag
and tells me to have the doctors
increase her pain medicine.
I pray that Dotti will be better tomorrow.

8/22—4:30 P.M. THURSDAY

Dotti is drenched in urine
and other body fluids
and too tired and dehydrated
to cat or exercise.
The borne health care nurse
cleans Dotti's dressings
and changes her ostomies.
As I watch her sleep,
her skin waxen, her arms bony,
I worry that she may not awaken.
Yet I must maintain hope for her
with whom I have shared this world.

8/23 Walnut Creek Nursing Home—12:15 P.M.

FRIDAY

As soon as we arrive,
the doctor says that Dotti may have
to leave the nursing home
if she has any serious problems,
such as high white blood cell count
or kidney failure. It scares me
that she's so lethargic
and can barely speak.
Her nurse thinks the pain
medicines are causing
Dotti's suspicious symptoms.
I cross my fingers and pray
that the nurse is right.

7:35 P.M. FRIDAY

Dotti's white blood cell count is 27.4.
A nurse tells me this means
she is in critical condition
and must be taken by ambulance
back to the James Cancer Hospital.
I sit in the empty nursing home lobby
hoping that Dotti's life can be saved.
She who endures so much pain,
she who is so thin, so drawn,
so weak and confused
is still here, still my wife, still my love
with a powerful urge to live!

8/24—11:25 A.M. SATURDAY

I fear losing Dotti
to a relentless killer
that does not know her name
that will never see feel or touch her
that will never share her insights
or feel her passion
a killer that may be
a monster of the deep
or a mutation encoded in Dotti's genes
a throw of the dice by fate or chance
or some unfeeling god
It is a plague on our house

11:30 P.M. SATURDAY

Driving through blinding rain
from Dayton to Columbus
ahead of the ambulance
taking Dotti back to the cancer hospital
because of her sky-high white blood cell count
praying that she be well
and that we survive this savage storm.

The James Cancer Hospital

8/25—5 P.M. SUNDAY

After being taken to the bathroom,
Dotti grimaces. When I ask her
what hurts, she replies,
"I've been through so much.
Everything hurts."
Her eyes closed,
her high cheekbones taut,
her lips locked in a grimace,
she tries to sleep through all
that she must bear to stay alive.

8/26—7 A.M. MONDAY

Today Dotti cannot eat or drink
until she has a procedure
to drain infected fluids from her bod.
While she rests in bed,
I jot down questions to ask
her medical team about her procedure.
Meanwhile the blazing sun
keeps rising in the eastern sky.

6:10 P.M. MONDAY

Dr. Fowler is enraged because
Dotti has still not had her
abscesses drained by the CAT scan unit,
so he gets her in within minutes.
He tells Dotti that she will be well.
"Promise, Dr. Fowler. Promise."
When the chief resident tells her
all will be well, Dotti says,
"That means a lot coming from you."

8:35 P.M. MONDAY

Dotti's sister Geri and I walk behind
two black women who push Dotti's cart
to the CAT scan department.
Two large wooden doors open,
and Dotti disappears quickly
when the two doors close.
While I sit in a small vestibule,
what can I do but hope
that my wife who fights
so bravely will be cured.
Then this sad-faced doctor
sits next to me.
He says he did his best
but the abscesses are still there.
They are too thick to remove.
We are running out of options.
I watch him walk away
and disappear behind
two large closed wooden doors.

8/27—8:30 A.M. TUESDAY

While Dotti sleeps,
plasma drips down her IV tube
into her veins.
Lord heal her if you can.
Let the light of her life shine.
If this can't be, let her
be a star shining in the firmament.

There is a design or purpose to our lives
beyond our knowing but possible
to be imagined or believed.

8/28—11 A.M. WEDNESDAY

Dotti lies
next to the cuddly
brown fur teddy bear
that I :den bought her
at the gift shop.
Suddenly she cries out in pain.
The nurse comes into the room
and gives Dotti morphine.
When I ask the nurse
if Dotti can have valium,
she says that she can.

8/29 A.M. THURSDAY

After driving Geri to the Dayton Airport,
1 return to our Dayton house
and try to stop the mail
and newspaper delivery.
Thank goodness our friends the Reeces
have been watering our grass
and collecting our mail and newspapers
while Dotti and I have been in Columbus.
Before leaving, I pick the last
of our garden grown tomatoes
but forget them at a rest stop
on the drive back to the hospital.

8/31—7 A.M. SATURDAY

Last. night Dotti vomited
and then fell out of bed.
This morning she gets a CAT scan of her head.
Our little world is filled with dread.

Lord, no matter how much I pray to you
for Dotti's health to improve
she keeps having setbacks
that make me fear for her recovery,
but I want you to know
that both of us will fight on!

4:30 P.M. SATURDAY

Dr. Fowler walks grimly into the room.
Dotti's white blood cell count is way up
and her pulse rate is very high.
Although she has a CAT scan at 5 P.M.,
Dr. Fowler has decided
that she needs more surgery
to correct the obstruction of her bowel.
This may be the only way to save her life.
When I question a second operation,
Jenny says that she will leave
if Dotti doesn't have the surgery.
"I'm sorry, but I will," she says.
She stares at me with steely eyes.

7:30 P.M. SATURDAY

At last we get good news.
The CAT scan shows
no major bowel obstruction.
Dr. Fowler believes that
non-surgical radiological methods
can drain Dotti's infection.
Tonight we can tell ourselves
that with luck we will not need
more surgery to save her.

9/1—1:25 P.M. SUNDAY

Dr. Fowler tells Dotti
that antibiotics aren't making her better,
and the radiologist doesn't recommend
more CAT Scan needle draining.
"So today we may have to bite the bullet
and look inside you to see what's wrong
and correct the problem."
After Dotti requests to speak
alone with. Dr. Fowler,
I stand outside her room
and hear her ask him
if she will survive the surgery,
or if it will make things worse.
Are there any alternatives?

After Dr. Fowler answers Dotti's questions,
I return to the room.
When she asks him how old he is.
he replies, "Forty Four."
"You've got it," she says.
"I can do it today or tomorrow."
"Here's our deal, Dr. Fowler.
You'll do it today."
"Okay," he replies.
"We'll do it while there's light"

4 P.M. SUNDAY

Once more I read the great voices
of our poetry: Yeats, Frost, Stevens,
Hardy, Hopkins, and other poets
I have loved since I was a boy
lost in the woods or walking
alone on the seashore dreaming
of the woman I would meet someday
who would lead me through fire and water.

Now years after she and I found each other,
she lies asleep, her pain numbed by drugs
after her surgery to find the source
of the enemy that punishes her body.
I feel her suffering and my sadness
as I read the great voices of our poetry.

9/2—11 A.M. MONDAY

Our marriage vows say that we
will cherish each other
in sickness and in health.
And so I cherish her,
my angelic love,
attacked by the cancer demon.
I swear we will be as one forever.

9/3—5 A.M. TUESDAY

Dotti sits in a chair in her room
and speaks with her nurse's aide
about going on a date in Minneapolis,
the place I left in the dead of winter
to find sunlight and her
in the blazing Arizona desert
where she showed me how fertile
the desert was at night
and in the morning and how we
too could make crops grow.
When the nurse asks if I
was her date in Minneapolis,
Dotti smiles and says, "Of course."

9/4—9 A.M. WEDNESDAY

Lord, Lord, Dotti's white blood cell count
is down again to 19.
Lord, Lord, whoever you are,
please continue to heal Dotti.
Please bring down her heart rate
and unplug her bowel.
Lord, Lord, whoever you are,
and skeptical as I am,
I call upon you in my time of need.

11:15 A.M.

When Dotti's chief resident
finds her incision is leaking,
she uses a small pliers
to remove some of the sutures.
After she cleans, disinfects,
and dries the tissue around the wound,
she inserts a gauze bandage to the site.
Dotti's medical team and I
surround her bed.
I try to read their faces
for significant signs.

9/5—1 P.M. THURSDAY

Dotti's temperature is normal.
Her blood pressure and oxygen rates are good.
And her white blood cell count has
come down for the third straight day.
Her team is elated because last night
she passed some stool during her enema.
Why then is she so pale and tired?
Has she not heard her own good news?

9/6—8:30 A.M. FRIDAY

I am at Wright State
waiting for the secretary to show up
so I can check my mail.
I feel out of place and guilty
for being here because
I'm so used to being with Dotti
at the James Cancer Hospital.
When I call her from my office,
she says, "Hi lovey."

Driving back to Columbus from Dayton,
I watch the flat, parched land flash by.
When I get back to the hospital
and walk into Dotti's room,
her smile captivates me.
How healing is her smile.
It is redemption's light.

9/7—8:10 A.M. SATURDAY

After falling over her bed railing,
determined to go to the bathroom,
Dotti wears pain's face

Listen to Debussy my love
and sleep through the pain
that plagues you.
Wherever you go I shall follow
over the earth and beyond its shores
to the point where earth
and sky and sun converge.

3 P.M. SATURDAY

Four walks in one day: a record for Dotti.
During the first two walks
she went twice
around the nurses's station.
If we can get her to stop
falling on her way to the bathroom,
and her appetite returns,
she'll be on her way
to recovery on our shared journey.

9/8—2 P.M. SUNDAY

From her hospital bed
Dotti looks up at me and says,
"All I need is your acceptance.
That's all I need and care about."
"You have it," I reply.

9/9—9 P.M. MONDAY

Come on Jesus enter our room.
Lay your healing hands on Dotti, my wife,
and make her strong and healthy
as she was before her illness.
Since we Jews and Christians
share the same roots,
why not stick together.
Our law can use your faith
and vice versa
and there's no monopoly on God.
He/She belongs to everyone
who inhabits the earth.
Come on Jesus enter our room.
Lay your healing hands on Dotti, my wife.

9/10 — 8:30 A.M. TUESDAY

Dotti sits in her recliner
sleeping with her mouth open
clutching her black pain button.

9/11—9:10 P.M. WEDNESDAY

Dotti sleeps with two fingers in her mouth
and her knees raised high.
Her body is learning to live with pain
that turns her smile to a smirk.

9/12—3:30 P.M. THURSDAY

I am not afraid (now)
I accept what is (now)
Death is part of life
and may not be
an end but a beginning
of a new life
new possibilities
where fire and water
earth and sky
are one
and indivisible

The Walnut Hills Nursing Home

9/13—8 A.M. FRIDAY

Nurses, nurses, what would we do without nurses?
All sick people need nurses.
Even healthy people feel better
with a nurse around to nurture them.
And why is it that so many of the best nurses
are overweight? Does their extra weight
make them more matronly?
Maybe our desire for nurses goes back
to our mother's womb and sucking her breasts.
Everyone knows that mother's milk
is sweet and nourishing.
Of course, the promised land had milk
as well as honey. If I were rich,
I'd hire an around the clock nurse
and not look back!

9/14 SATURDAY

I can't drive myself crazy
about every nuance of Dotti's health.
Now it's an elevated temperature
that could mean she has
another infection. But the hell with it.
After the last infection caused her
to be hospitalized for three weeks
and undergo a second surgery,
I'm going to remain calm, cool,
stoic, tough no matter what.
I swear it!

We live out our marriage vows
two imperfect people who complement
each other in the act of sharing
and who can be proud of
two exceptional daughters
who nurture us in this tough time
when Dotti's body is under assault
and I am here to help her
because I am her husband for life.

9/15 SUNDAY

Many years ago Dotti taught me
not to be afraid of loving and being
loved by her who bore me
over rippling waves from shore
to shore until we rested
in our arms and hands.
Now she takes me on another journey
that we cannot prepare for
although it cannot be sidestepped.
It is as omnipresent and mysterious
as the sky asking nothing
and yet everything of us.

9/16—6:30 A.M. MONDAY

Today begins with hope.
You have been "a brave girl"
as my mother would have said.
Or as I say: you are my heroine,
my valiant partner fighting to live.
In your sickness your sweet soul
sings, and I listen.

Listen to the great music of the life force
the rhythms of creation
the sea's ceaseless motion
the season's coming and going
the pulse tapping its vital code
this and so much more you are
alive to at this instant now.

9/17—3:30 A.M. TUESDAY

When I walk down your hallway,
the nurse runs up to me
and says that Dotti's been
asking for me because
she is leaking stool
through her vaginal opening.
She's already terrified
of her elevated temperature
and high white blood cell count.
Now there's a new crisis.
In fact, her life has been
in crisis for months now.

9/18—12:10 P.M. WEDNESDAY

Dotti and I and our children are in hell.
She has suffered still
another terrible setback.
I don't know how much more
she can suffer or when
to tell the doctors ENOUGH.
LET MY WIFE GO TO A PEACEFUL PLACE.

Lord she has endured so much.
Is it not time to call a halt
to tubes, needles, antibiotics,
painkillers, anesthetics, the surgeon's knife?
My love 1 want to live side by side
and hand in hand with you forever.
And I will. I have that faith.
But now we must decide how you
will cross that wide river.

9/19—11:15 A.M. THURSDAY

Dotti tells us today
that she has had enough;
she just wants to be comfortable.
And for the first time in weeks
she seems at peace,
as if a great burden
has been lifted from her:
her poor sick body.
And her soul can rise and sing.
Though I weep and weep
because I will miss her so much,
I too feel a sense of peace
because I know that her earthly
suffering will soon cease,
and she will live among the angels.

9/20—9:25 A.M. FRIDAY

How precious each second seems
now that Dotti lies so close to death.
Our thirty five years fly by.
We have so little time to speak the words
that we will never get to say again:
words of love and sadness and loss.
And most of all: Goodby my love
my one and only life-sustaining love.
Thank you for all that you have given to me.
Hospice of Dayton

9/21 SATURDAY

Jennifer and Eden said
that they would go to Dayton
and get you into a wonderful place
and they did.
Your final home is filled with light.
A s you begin to live your last days,
rest my love and be comfortable
while your loved ones try to accept
and affirm your passing.
Then we must and will
celebrate your life.

9/22 SUNDAY

Despite Dotti's bravery
and her doctors' tenacity
Isee her dying from cancer's
assault on her body.
Though I will mourn
her loss always,
I will live on for now
and watch her soul's soaring
victory over death.

9/23 MONDAY

I will never be ready for Dotti's death
Yet I need not worry
For she will always be with me
Helping me, guiding me, encouraging me
To be and do my best.
We found each other far from home
And learned to make a place
For ourselves within each other
Settling down midway between
Where we had met and where we had
Started out on our separate journeys.
Now Dotti is preparing to leave me,
But I pray that she knows
That I will always be with her
Wherever she may be.

9/24—8 A.M. Tuesday

My love, ducks and birds and squirrels
congregate at your window.
Do you see them, my love?
They are here to take you to the place
where you and your aunt May and your
grandfather Bill and other loved ones
will live in a heavenly estate
beyond the means of the richest C.E.O.

Dotti lies on her bed
at the edge of the hospice veranda
looking out at a rose garden
and beyond the garden
at trees surrounding
a pond with ducks honking
and birds swooping around us.
Because she is so frail
and her skin is so sallow,
I pray that she has not yet reached
death's long deep sleep.
Suddenly four ducks flapping
their wings soar over us.

9/25—2:55 WEDNESDAY

My love, your body may die
but your soul will live
in a tree house in heaven
where the sun shines
and angels sing you to sleep.
Since you have always shown
me the way, I will follow
and find you, and we
will live as one soul
smiling down upon the earth.

5:10 P.M. WEDNESDAY

As he blows smoke in my face,
the eucharistic minister
tells me he's somewhere
between a nasty separation
and a bitter divorce
from the mother of his seven children.
While she broods within herself,
he has a huge singles support group
and a girlfriend to sustain him.
His lizard eyes have a peripheral focus
away from me, but he won't take a hint
and leave me to my private grief.
"I'm a writer and I like to write,
so I'll see you later," I say.
"I don't know about your God,"
he replies, "but mine has brought me
many beautiful moments."
"I know," I tell him, and "Goodby."

9/26—4:35 P.M. THURSDAY

In this quiet peaceful place
where my wife lies dying,
I look through windows at trees,
flowers, bushes, bird feeders,
and I wonder if I am dreaming.
But feeling how tense I am,
I know that I am awake
and my wife lies dying.
Although I can't change that fact,
I can hope and pray
that when she dies her soul
will soar far above the earth
on her journey to paradise.

9/27—10:05 A.M. FRIDAY

Even as she lies dying
Dotti's face is serene
and perfectly modeled
as if painted by Matisse,
Degas, or Valasquez.
Her diamond earrings shine
beneath her long brown hair.
Her large eyes green and hazy
focus on some place
deep within her and yet faraway
where she is preparing to go.
It is too mysterious for words,
yet she will show me the way
for she has always been my teacher.

9/28—7 P.M. SATURDAY

I am going to miss you, my earthly love,
and I will grieve for your earthly loss.
But you and I will always hold hands,
kiss, and speak of what matters most to us.
You have long been a part of me,
a part of all that I see, hear, taste,
touch, smell, and think about the world
that we were born into by parents
we never picked whom fate chose
to create us and give us our names.
You will always walk beside me
as I go on to discover what I can
about the mystery of being here:
holding your hand, kissing your lips,
looking into your eyes, my love.

9/29—3:30 P.M. SUNDAY

Bless you my dying love
During your last earthly moments
May your spirit's light
Always illuminate your loved ones
And give us peace And may you always know
Serenity in your new life.

9/30—9:25 A.M. MONDAY

My love, I have been with you
almost around the clock
for forty eight hours now.
I await your passing
with a sense of calmness and peace,
because I know we have both done
all that we can to live out our fate
as a couple with devotion and dignity.

11:50 A.M.

Dotti's breathing has almost stopped.
Her skin is cold and clammy.
Her eyes are red,
and her pupils turn inward.
I kiss her and whisper in her ear
that she is going to heaven
and I will follow her.
She has almost stopped breathing.
Her eyes open and peer at me.
Then she gasps and lies
silently and in repose.
I know her soul has risen above
her body's earthly suffering.

www.ingramcontent.com/pod-product-compliance
Lightning Source LLC
LaVergne TN
LVHW011944070526
838202LV00054B/4787